Helmeted
warrior

Mangoes and papayas

Double-hulled canoe

PLATE 1

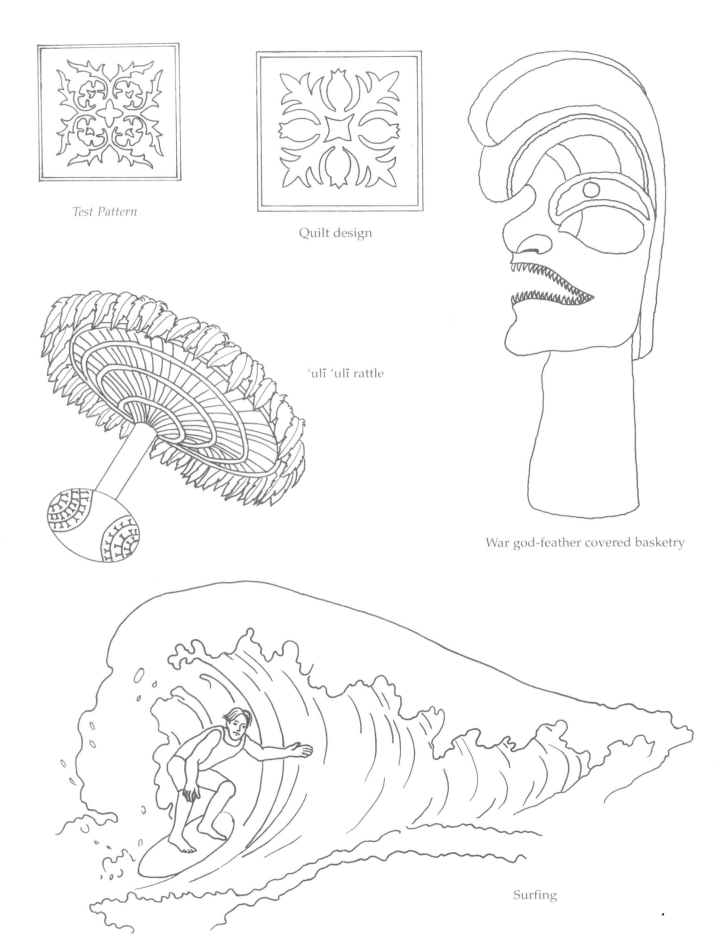

Test Pattern

Quilt design

'ulī 'ulī rattle

War god-feather covered basketry

Surfing

PLATE 2

Print design for kapa cloth

Kū the war god
(carved wood)

Beach Scene

PLATE 3

Hawaii's first royal coat-of-arms

PLATE 4

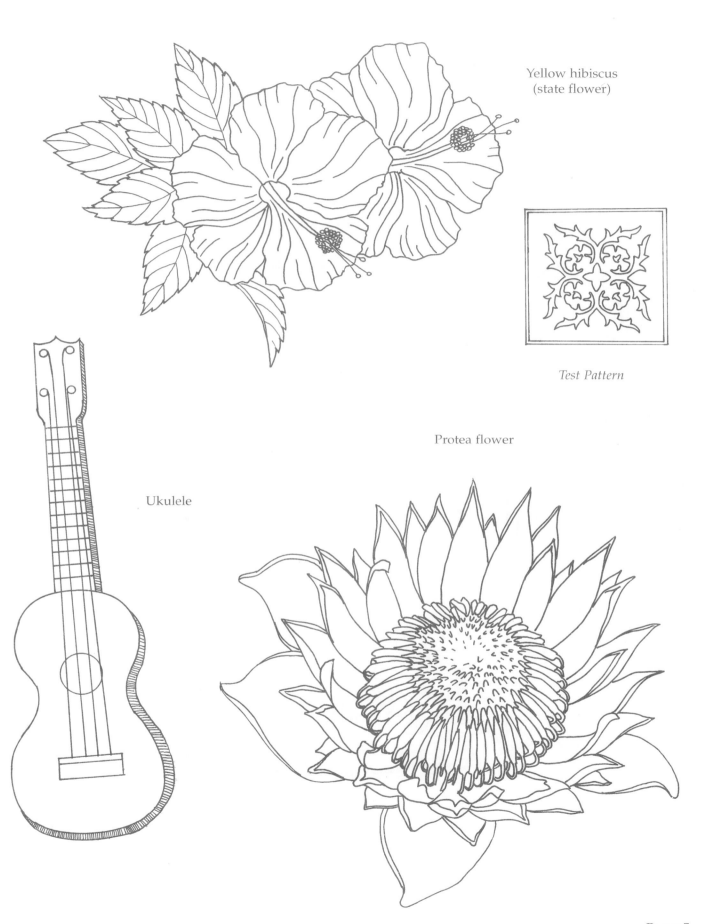

Yellow hibiscus
(state flower)

Test Pattern

Ukulele

Protea flower

PLATE 5

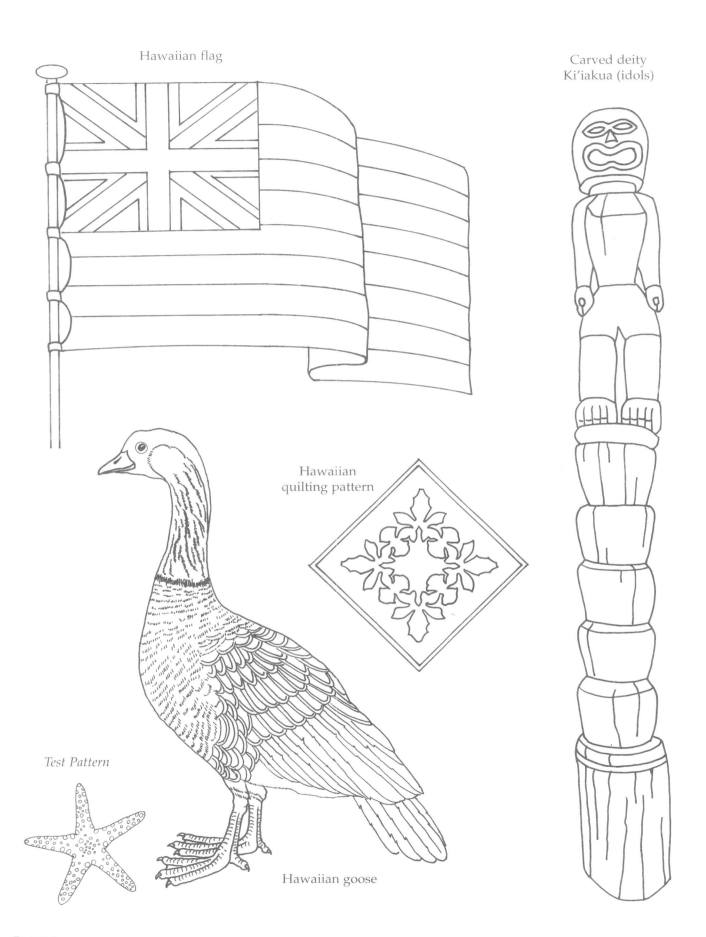

Hawaiian flag

Carved deity
Ki'iakua (idols)

Hawaiian
quilting pattern

Test Pattern

Hawaiian goose

PLATE 6

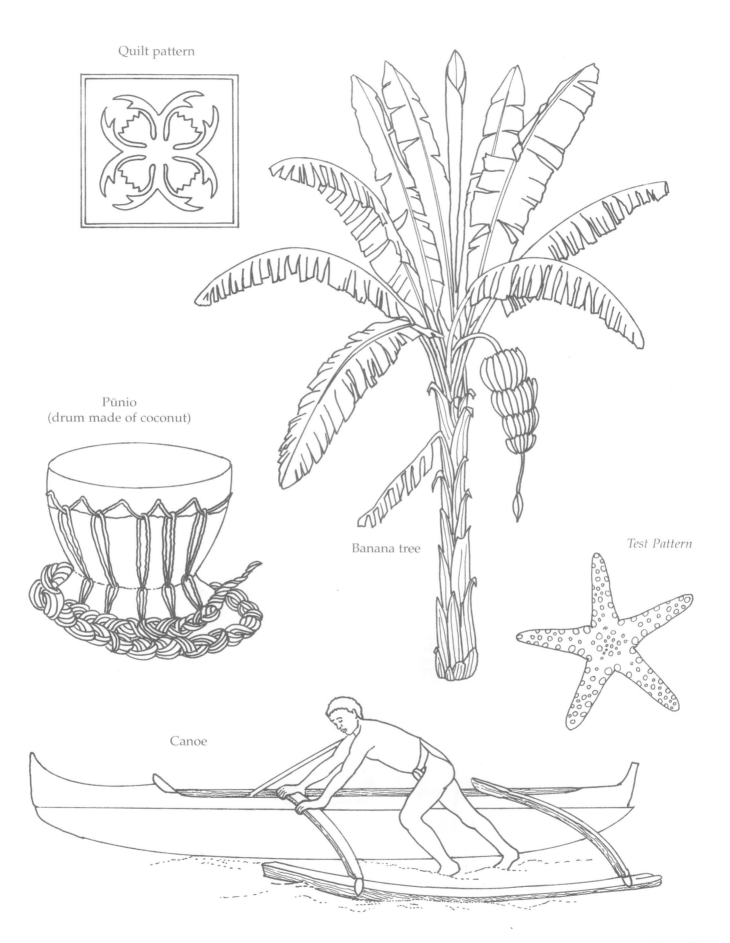

Quilt pattern

Pūnio
(drum made of coconut)

Banana tree

Test Pattern

Canoe

PLATE 7

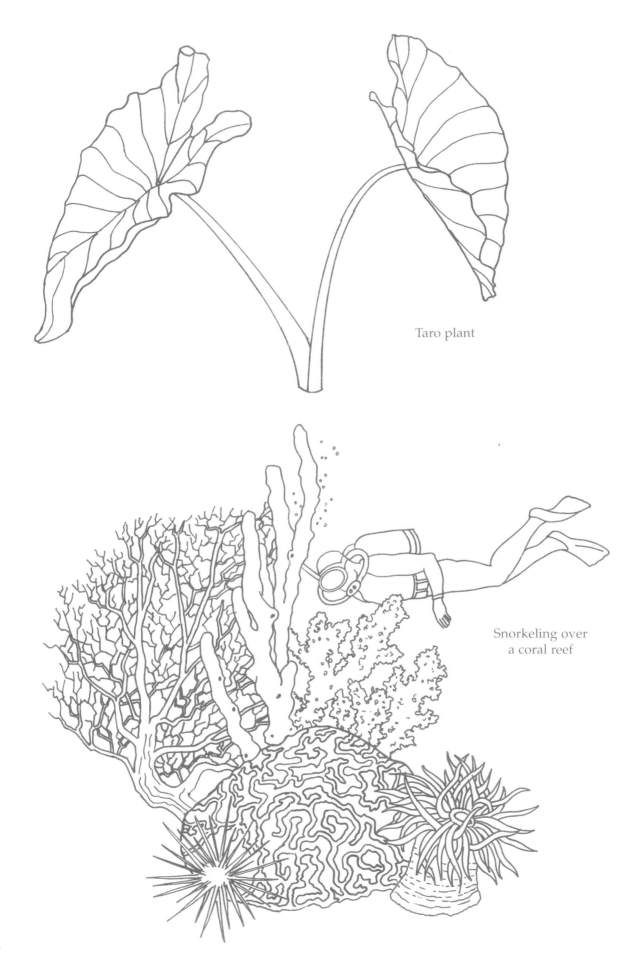

Taro plant

Snorkeling over
a coral reef

PLATE 8

Map of Hawaiian Islands

Test Pattern

PLATE 9

Ōhi ʻa lehua tree

Kūkaʻilimoku
(feather-covered basketry)

Iiwi honeycreeper

Test Pattern

PLATE 10

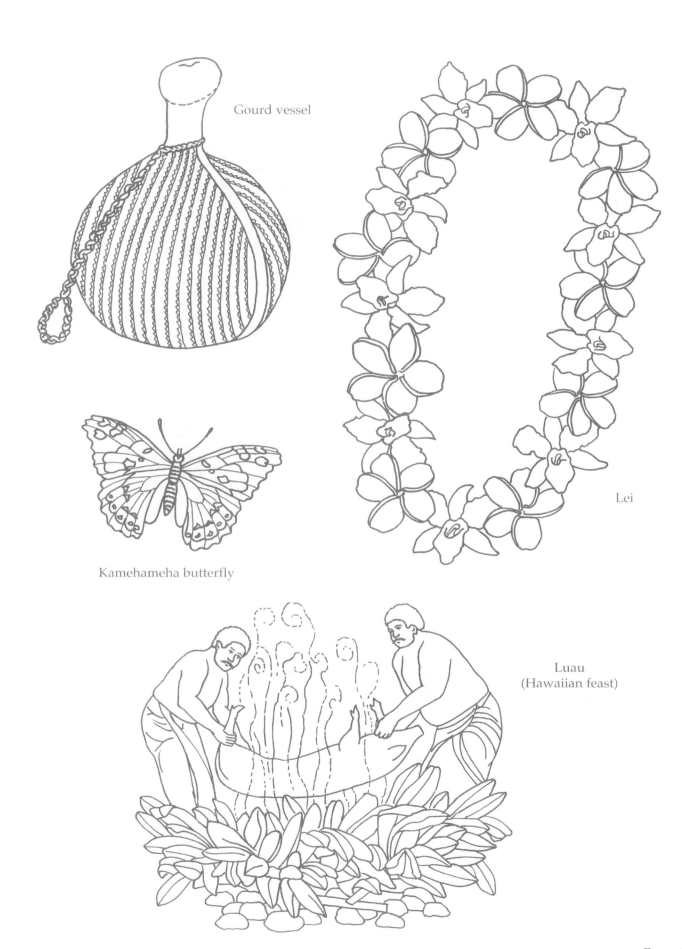

Gourd vessel

Lei

Kamehameha butterfly

Luau
(Hawaiian feast)

PLATE 11

Petroglyphs

PLATE 12

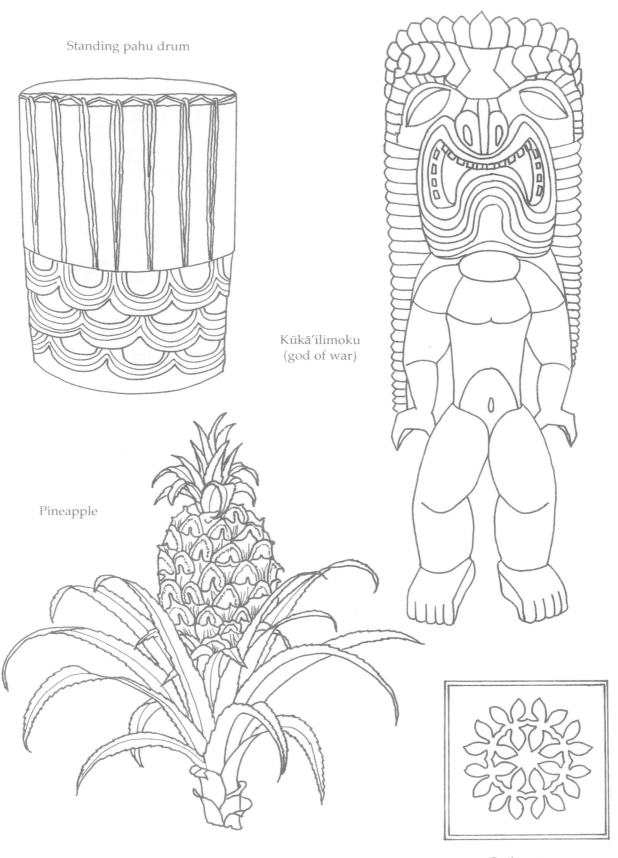

Standing pahu drum

Kūkā'ilimoku
(god of war)

Pineapple

Quilt pattern

PLATE 13

Hawaiian ʻoʻo

Moorish idol

Silversword / ʻāhinahina

PLATE 14

Test Pattern

Hawaiian girl wearing
traditional bark cloth
"Kapa" costume

Orchid

Test Pattern

Green sea turtle

PLATE 15

Diamond Head

Test Pattern

Waikiki Beach

PLATE 16

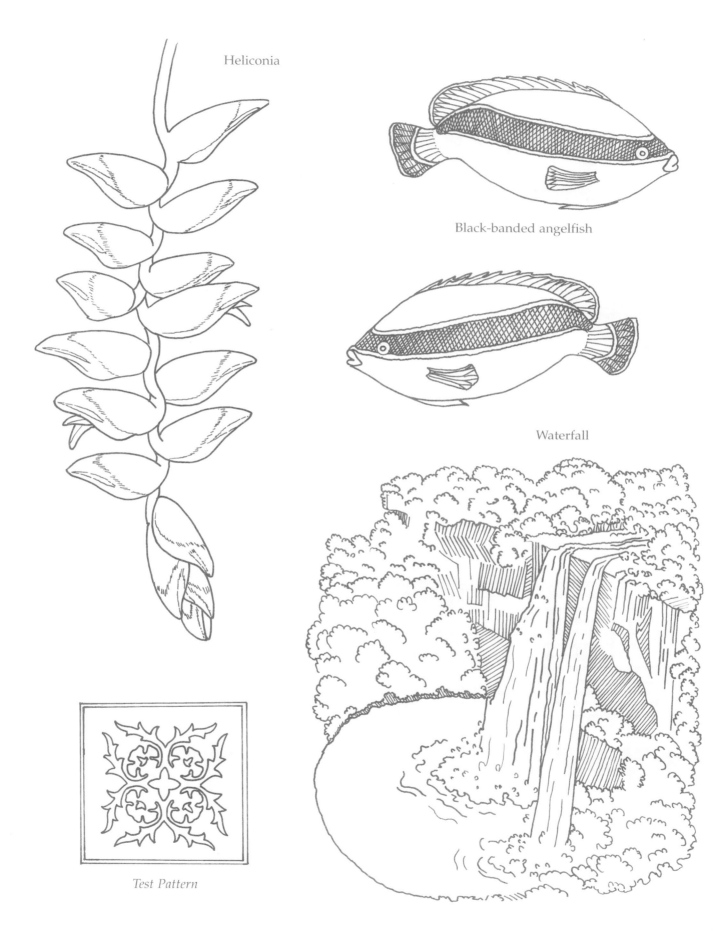

Heliconia

Black-banded angelfish

Waterfall

Test Pattern

PLATE 17

Red ginger

Quilt pattern

Hula
dancer

Starfish

PLATE 18

Hawaiian
spinner dolphin

Akohekohe
(crested honeycreeper)

Test Pattern

Oahu tree snail

PLATE 19

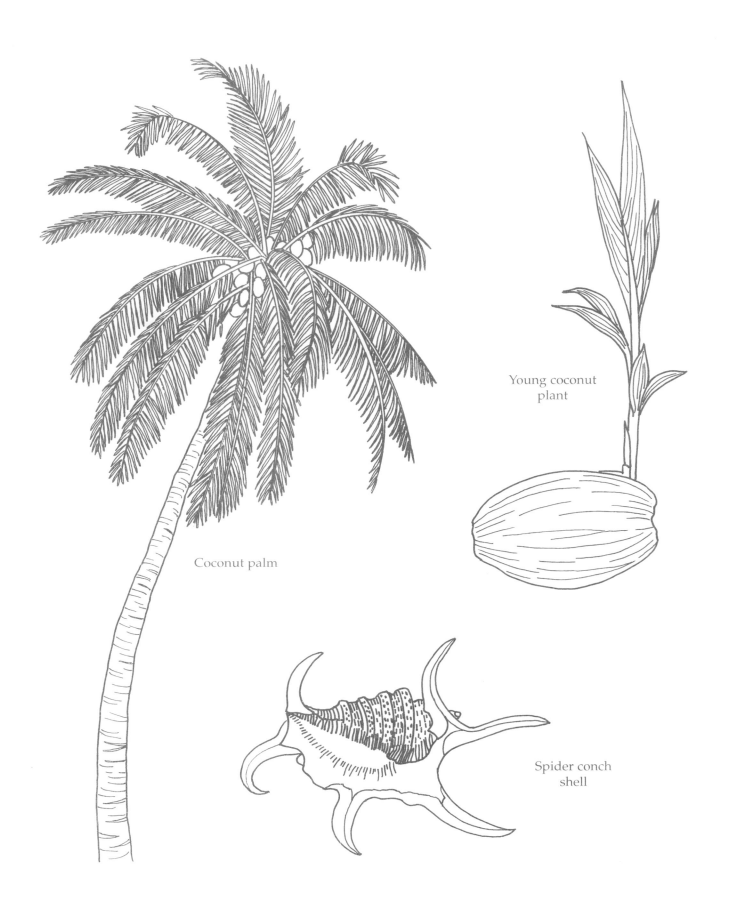

Young coconut
plant

Coconut palm

Spider conch
shell

PLATE 20

Carved figure

Ceremonial staff

Ti

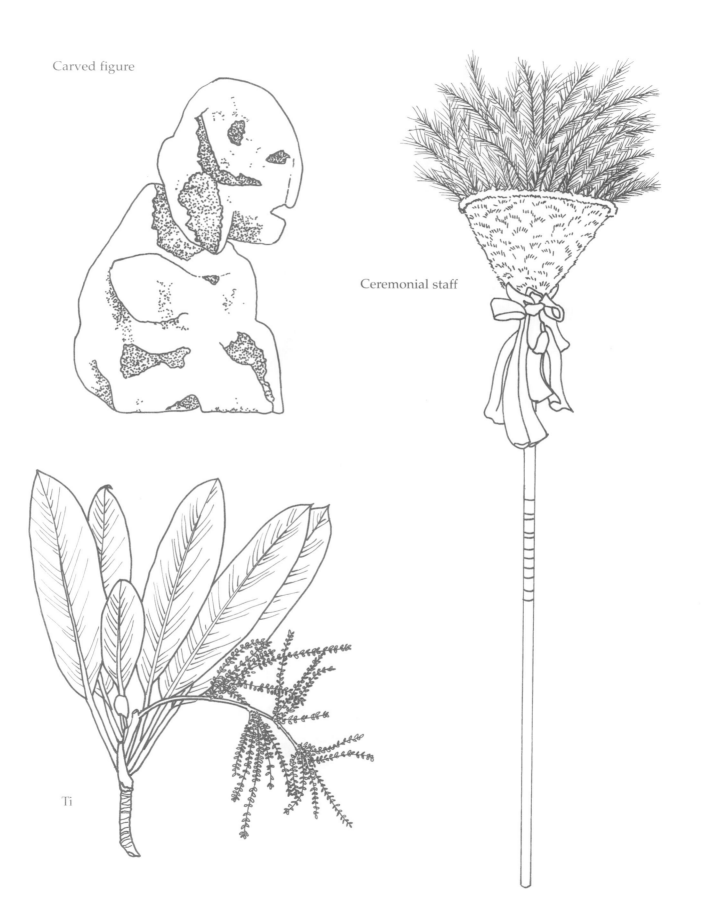

PLATE 21

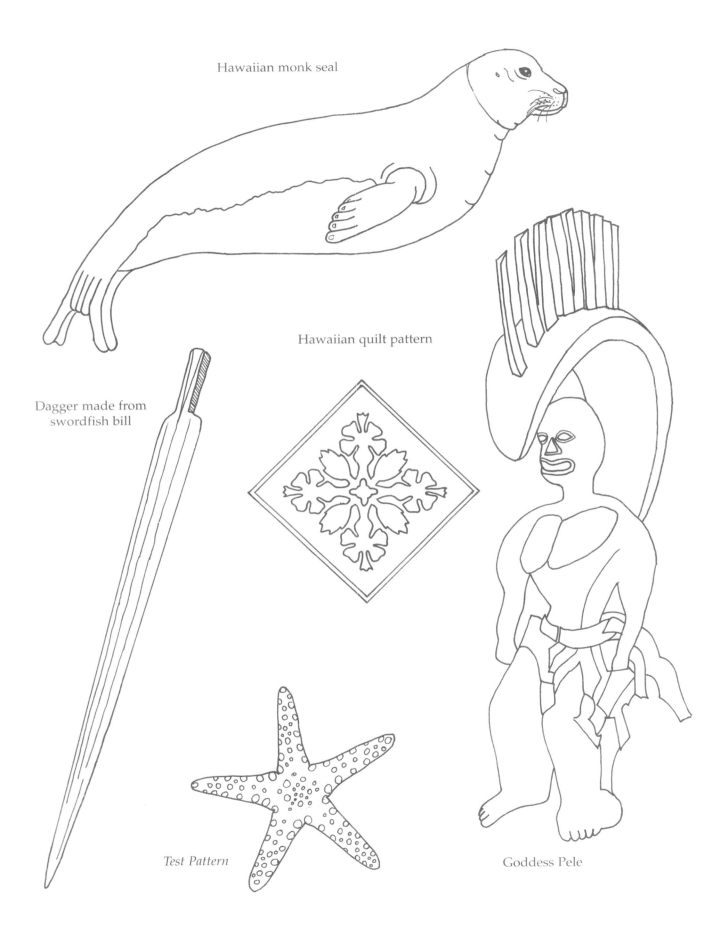

Hawaiian monk seal

Hawaiian quilt pattern

Dagger made from
swordfish bill

Test Pattern

Goddess Pele

PLATE 22

State tree: kukui
(candlenut tree)

Ipu heke
(percussion instrument)

Queen Ka'ahumanu

PLATE 23

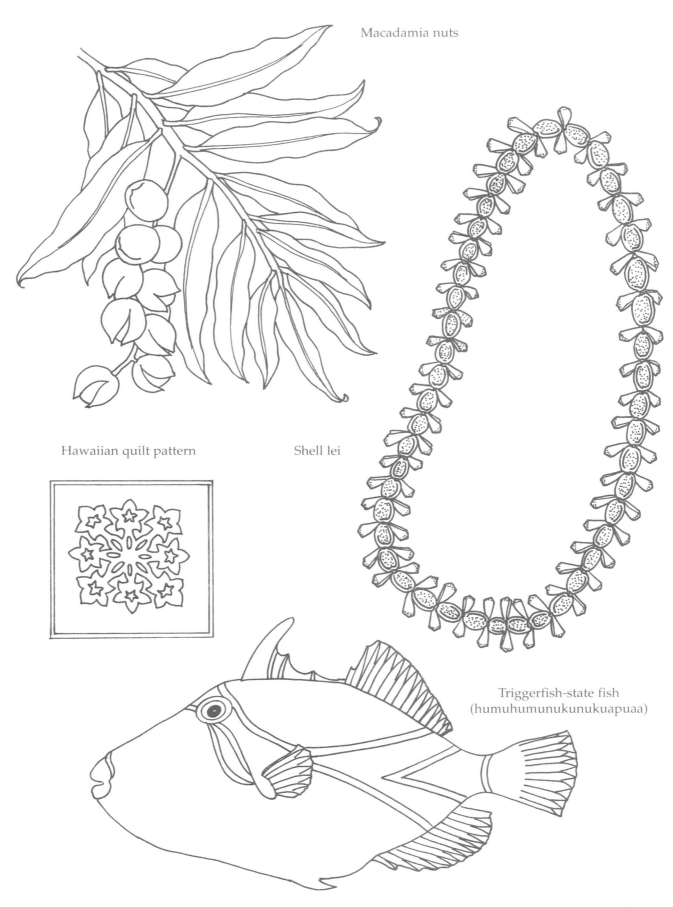

Macadamia nuts

Hawaiian quilt pattern

Shell lei

Triggerfish-state fish
(humuhumunukunukuapuaa)

PLATE 24